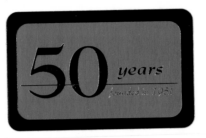

PRESENTED BY

William Bridges
in honor of

Judy Windham

2002

WESTMINSTER SCHOOLS   SMYTHE GAMBRELL LIBRARY

STAGECOACH

The Ride of a Century

By A. Richard Mansir

Charlesbridge

For Anne, whose initials *AU* stand for solid gold. — ARM

The editors would like to thank Wells Fargo Historical Services, San Francisco, and Lee Swanson, the Historic Coordinator at Longfellow's Wayside Inn in Sudbury, Massachusetts.

Wells Fargo Trademarks are registered trademarks of Wells Fargo & Company and are used under license to Charlesbridge Publishing, Inc. Wells Fargo illustrations and photographs used with express permission.

Published by Charlesbridge Publishing, 85 Main Street, Watertown, MA 02472 • (617) 926-0329
• http://www.charlesbridge.com

Printed in the United States of America
10 9 8 7 6 5 4 3 2 1

Library of Congress Cataloging-in-Publication Data
Mansir, A. Richard.
    Stagecoach: the ride of a century / text and illustrations by A. Richard Mansir.
    p.   cm. - (Building America series)
    Includes index.
    Summary: Recounts the history of the stagecoach in America from the early days of the
Republic to the westward expansion, using illustrations, historical documents, maps, and
fictional diary entries.
    ISBN 1-57091-955-0 (softcover). ISBN 1-57091-960-7 (reinforced fpr library use)
    1. Coaching - United States - History - Juvenile literature. 2. Travel - United States - History -
Juvenile literature. 3. Roads - United States - History - Juvenile literature. [1. Coaching - History.
2. Transportation - History.] I. Title. II. Series: Building America series (Watertown, Mass.)

HE5747.M35 1998
388.3'228'0973 - dc21   98-36315

"Hee-yuh!" shouts the stagecoach driver when he sees the pistol-waving outlaws. He snaps the reins and the horses gallop so fast that the coach leaves the outlaws behind in a cloud of dust. The grateful passengers cheer as the coach thunders down the road.

Can you imagine yourself riding in this stagecoach, bouncing up and down with all the other passengers? Imagine the feel of the leather and the smell of the horses. Hear the driver shouting and the wooden wheels clattering as the horses' hoofbeats slow to a steady clip-clop.

Outside your window is a great new country, filled with plants and animals you have never seen before. You might travel through boggy marshes, grassy prairies, parched deserts, and snowy mountains. Is this an incredible adventure or a hopeless nightmare? It depends on your point of view.

Josh Biddle's Diary

Boston to New York, Day 1   October 17, 1830

Soon after we set out on the Post Road, it started raining. Not just raining, but pouring. The leather window shades didn't stop the rain from coming in, and the roof leaked. In a little while, I was completely soaked.

I held my breath as we started down a steep, muddy hill. The coach was slipping sideways at each curve. When we hit a bump, the coach stopped, and I tumbled into the front seat. I pulled myself up to a window and looked out.

The coach was tipped to one side with its wheels stuck in deep mud.

When the coach got stuck, passengers helped. They shoved logs and branches under the coach's big back wheels. Then they pushed and strained until the coach rolled slowly back onto solid ground.

Riding a Coach in Stages

Before cars, trains, and planes, a stagecoach was the best way to travel and to send mail. A stagecoach divided a long distance into a series of short parts, called stages. New horses, and sometimes new drivers, took over at the beginning of each stage.

Stagecoaches were an important part of American life for more than 100 years. It is hard to imagine how the United States would have developed without them.

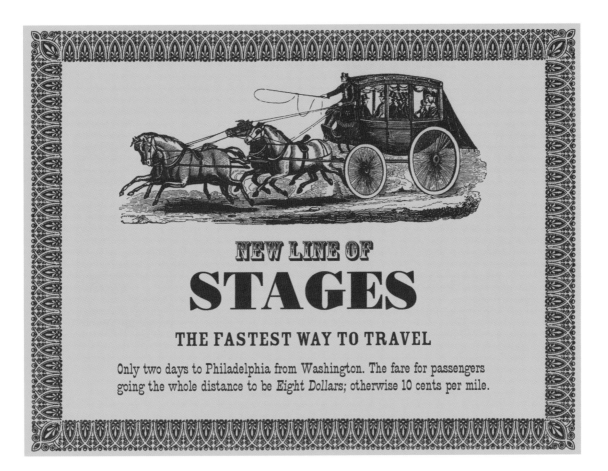

NEW LINE OF

STAGES

THE FASTEST WAY TO TRAVEL

Only two days to Philadelphia from Washington. The fare for passengers going the whole distance to be *Eight Dollars*; otherwise 10 cents per mile.

The Stagecoach in Colonial Days

In the 1600s, it was very difficult to get from town to town. You might walk or ride a horse over narrow, winding trails through hilly forests and swamps. Few roads in the Thirteen Colonies were good enough for any kind of wheels.

Conditions in the American colonies gradually improved after 1700. Stage wagons and stagecoaches began carrying people and packages between large cities.

How was riding in a stagecoach different from riding in a car?

No pavement
Early roads were rough dirt paths. Mud, rocks, potholes, and fallen trees made travel difficult and dangerous.

No seatbelts
With nothing to hold you in your seat, a deep rut or big bump could make you bounce around or crash into other passengers.

Leather windows
Most coach windows were covered with leather shades that could be unrolled and buckled to the walls. Glass windows would have shattered on bad roads.

Horse power
A team of horses pulled the coach, and they needed special care, food, and handling. If the driver lost control, the horses could run away with the coach.

Horses are not as strong as car engines. A stagecoach had the pulling power of six horses. The weakest car in America today has a 55 horsepower engine. Imagine a stagecoach hitched up to 55 horses!

Linking a New Nation

Stagecoach travel became common after the Revolutionary War (1775-1783), when the colonies won their independence from Great Britain. Stagecoaches carried young and old, rich and poor, on roads linking the new states. Traveling statesmen bumped knees with farmers, teachers, and merchants.

People needed more mail, too. They had just finished fighting for a new country, and now they wanted to read about their new leaders and laws. Americans moving west wanted to keep in touch with their families and friends who stayed behind.

Benjamin Franklin set out to organize the country's first postal system. He had to decide on the best way to distribute letters and newspapers to the news-hungry public. The stagecoach seemed to be the answer.

Stagecoaches could travel about 10 miles an hour, twice as fast as a wagon or a person on foot. A rider on a galloping horse could go faster, but could not carry much. Coaches could carry more mail, and they could keep the mail dry and safe. Stagecoaches began carrying the mail in 1785.

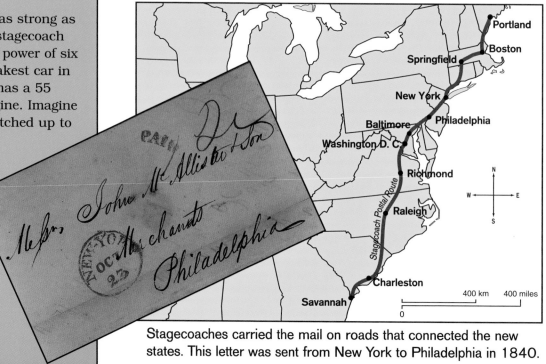

Stagecoaches carried the mail on roads that connected the new states. This letter was sent from New York to Philadelphia in 1840.

Josh's Journey Continues

Boston to New York, Day 1   October 17, 1830

It was 9 o'clock at night by the time our coach rumbled to a stop at the inn. Inside, a fire roared in a huge fireplace, making the walls and low ceiling glow. We ate at a long table by the fire. The steaming pumpkin, squash, onions, beef, pork, and bread were delicious. The best part was washing it all down with a mug of hot apple cider. Pa said it cost a lot of money – 40 cents – but I think it was worth it.

Passengers traveling with the mail might spend the night at a wayside inn. When the coach was about a mile from the inn, the driver blew on a trumpet. The number of blasts told the innkeeper how many passengers would be arriving.

After passengers ate, they went to sleep with all their clothes on except their shoes. Three to four people might sleep in the same bed. They would be awakened in the middle of the night if another traveler climbed into the bed. Sometimes there was no room left, and people had to sleep on the floor.

The initials and dates on this sign tell when different innkeepers took over the inn.

Josh's Journey Continues

Boston to New York, Day 2   October 18, 1830

We were eating breakfast at 5AM when the driver shouted, "Coach is leaving in five minutes! Anyone who's not on board gets left behind!"

Pa and I got the window seats and watched other passengers come running. One man had just jumped out of bed. He had his wig and hat in one hand and his boots under his arm. The coach waited for no one!

"Whope, git!" the driver shouted to the horses. "Come up, Blaze and Thunder! Smokey and Samson! Shorty and Star!"

Off we went! I stuck my head out the window and waved at people as we flew past. I wonder if they know this coach goes all the way to New York. Only three more days until we get there!

Blaze

Stepping Lively in the East

By 1820, a network of improved roads linked cities and towns throughout the East. These roads were called turnpikes, or tollroads. Stagecoach companies paid tolls to landowners who would keep the roads passable. The landowners removed snow in the winter, cut back bushes in the summer, and filled in potholes in the spring. They also cleared away fallen trees and moved big rocks.

Wherever decent roads went, stagecoaches followed. By 1840, you could travel west by stagecoach from Massachusetts to the Mississippi River, or south from Maine to Georgia.

Day and night, summer and winter, coaches rushed along the turnpikes. Along their routes, wayside inns blossomed. The inns competed for customers by offering fine food and comfortable lodging. Some inns even offered free meals, and it became easy to get a bed all to yourself.

Competing stagecoach companies boasted that they had the best rides. They bought bigger and better coaches that could go faster along the turnpikes. Competition was so fierce that sometimes two drivers would race between towns, their coaches scraping together as the drivers tried to force each other off the road.

Emily Cookson's Diary

Columbus, Ohio   January 15, 1849

I was in the general store today when Mr. Newman came bounding in. Out of breath and waving a letter in the air, he shouted to the entire store: "G-g-gold in Californy! They found gold in Californy!"

Gold Rush!
The Stagecoach in California

By the mid-1800s, railroads were replacing stagecoaches in the East. Meanwhile, in the West, the discovery of gold in California made stagecoaches very important.

In early 1848, James Marshall was building a sawmill for John Sutter on the American River. One morning, he found a shiny yellow nugget in the stream. He had discovered gold!

In December of 1848, President James Polk announced the discovery of gold to the nation. Even people who had laughed at the rumors of gold now dreamed of going to California. "Gold Fever" was spreading fast.

In 1849, thousands of gold-seekers, called Forty-niners, traveled west. Butchers and grocers closed their shops, sailors left their boats, and farmers left their farms. There was gold in California! Everyone expected to make a fortune.

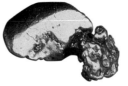

In the early days of the Gold Rush, gold nuggets could be found in streambeds. The United States government bought gold to make it into coins. These are an actual-size $50 gold piece and three gold nuggets.

The fastest route to California took months. Some people sailed from the east coast to get to Central America. There they walked or rode mules for two days through the jungle, then waited for a boat to take them up the coast to California. To avoid jungle diseases such as malaria and cholera, some people sailed all around South America. Other travelers went overland, making the six- to eight-month trip by horseback or wagon.

A few Forty-niners did strike it rich in the gold fields. Many others made their fortunes by providing the tools, clothing, food, and supplies the miners needed. Soon there were towns filled with hastily built rooming houses, stores, and other services.

Life in the mining towns was often dangerous. One businessman, Jim Birch, realized miners needed a way to get their gold to banks safely. He started the California Stage Company. Within five years, Birch was a millionaire. He owned 80 stagecoaches, 125 wagons, and more than 1,000 horses and mules.

Soon, a thriving stagecoach business grew up in California. Stagecoaches criss-crossed the roads between mines and towns, carrying miners, money, and bags of gold.

West of Tipton, Missouri   **December 15, 1858**

We're on our way to California at last! Pa wrote a letter asking us to join him in San Francisco. Ma and I packed our bags, said goodbye to everyone, and caught the train from St. Louis to Tipton. In Tipton, we bought tickets for the Butterfield Stage for $200 each. People used to laugh at the idea of a stagecoach going all the way out west, but we're on our way there now!

The First Cross-Country Stage Route

A year after the Gold Rush, there were enough Americans in California for it to become a state. Californians wanted weekly newspapers and mail from loved ones. Mail came only when a wagon train of new settlers arrived or when a ship reached port after sailing around South America. By then, the news was at least three months old.

In 1857, the government hired John Butterfield to start a stagecoach line to carry the mail. He bought a huge fleet of Concord Coaches, as well as lighter open-sided wagons to get through the desert quickly.

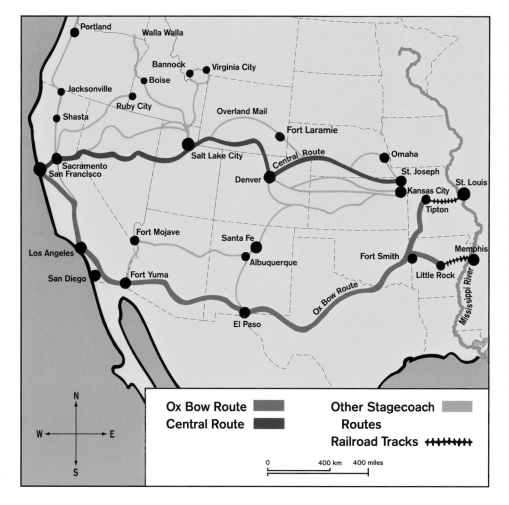

A bitter debate raged in Congress over the first cross-country stagecoach route. The North wanted a northern route, because they were afraid that the country's gold would fall into Southern hands if civil war began. The Southern states wanted to keep as much government business as possible.

Finally, Congress decided on the Ox Bow Route, which started in the North, but swung down into the South.

Butterfield spent millions of dollars organizing his overland mail route. He built trailside stations, bought horses, and hired about 800 drivers and stablehands.

Butterfield's stagecoaches began carrying mail on September 15, 1858. They crossed half a continent along the Ox Bow Route. From Tennessee and Missouri, this route swung south and west through 2,795 miles of plains and desert before reaching California. Butterfield was the first to link East to West with his transcontinental stagecoach line.

Less than three years later, Butterfield's southern route ended because of problems between the North and South. When the Civil War broke out in 1861, cross-country stagecoaches began traveling on the Central Route, which started farther north.

Wells, Fargo and Company®

The Central Route was run by Wells, Fargo and Company. In 1852, Wells Fargo opened a bank in San Francisco to help Gold Rush miners exchange their gold for money. Wells Fargo bankers became known for always paying a fair price for gold dust. In a frontier town full of troublemakers, miners were happy to find a bank they could trust.

Wells Fargo also ran a stagecoach service that transported gold, goods, and passengers throughout California. People said that this stagecoach service was better and faster than any other.

A Wells Fargo stagecoach was also safer. Guards rode with the drivers to protect the gold and mail. If bandits did manage to hold up the coach, Wells Fargo detectives tracked them down and put them in jail. Gold and money on a Wells Fargo stagecoach were guaranteed against robbery or loss.

Between 1852 and 1868, Wells, Fargo and Company grew quickly. In 1866, it became the biggest stagecoach company ever. From Kansas to California, and all along the West, Wells Fargo's bright red Concord Coaches rolled with mail, goods, and people.

Henry Wells
1805-1878

William G. Fargo
1818-1881

STAGECOACH RULES*

If you must eat or drink, share with others. To do otherwise makes you appear selfish and un-neighborly.

Buffalo robes are provided for your comfort during cold weather. Hogging robes will not be tolerated and the offender will be made to ride with the driver.

Don't snore loudly while sleeping or use your fellow passenger's shoulder for a pillow.

Firearms may be kept on your person for emergencies. Do not fire them for pleasure or shoot at wild animals as the sound riles the horses.

In the event of runaway horses, remain calm. Leaping from the coach in panic will leave you injured and at the mercy of the elements.

Gents guilty of unchivalrous behavior toward lady passengers will be put off the stage. It's a long walk back. A word to the wise is sufficient.

*According to legend

Stagecoach travelers often carried Colt revolvers for protection.

Building a Better Stagecoach

Famous for its strength and beauty, the Concord Coach was one of the few brand names known all across America.

Concord Coaches were made in Concord, New Hampshire, by a company called Abbot and Downing. The original 1827 design of the Concord Coach was so good that very few changes were made to it for 75 years.

Abbot and Downing knew that a chicken's egg can support many times its own weight. Therefore, they built their coach with strong, curving walls and used the lightest materials possible. They replaced many iron parts with wood. They steamed, shaped, and dried the wood until it was stronger than most iron.

Concord Coaches were built to last. People liked to tell the story of one that sank on a ship in San Francisco Bay. After a month under water, the coach was salvaged and dried out. It kept rolling for the next 50 years!

Another story was told about a Concord Coach that fell over a cliff. The front wheels came off and the door paintings were damaged, but the coach itself was unhurt.

How did the Concord Coach measure up?

Number of people one Concord could hold = 21
    (9 inside on 3 seats, and 12 on top)

Weight of one coach = 1,500-2,500 pounds

Cost of a coach = $1,200-1,500 on delivery

Height of a coach's rear wheels = 5 feet 1 inch

Height of a coach's front wheels = 3 feet 10 inches

Height of a coach = 8 feet 6 inches

Height of the driver's seat = 7 feet

"A Cradle on Wheels

Oiled leather **window shades** helped keep out snow, rain, and clouds of dust.

Mail was stored in the back area, or **boot**, which was covered with waterproofed leather.

The coach rested on thick leather straps called **thoroughbraces**. The coach could rock back and forth on these straps like a rocking horse. Mark Twain wrote that it was as comfortable as a "cradle on wheels."

The World-Famous Concord Coach

The **body** of a Concord Coach was usually painted bright red and varnished so that it shone like a mirror.

Across the top, the **name of the company** that bought the coach was painted in gold leaf.

From the **driver's box,** the driver handled four to six horses and had a clear view of the road ahead.

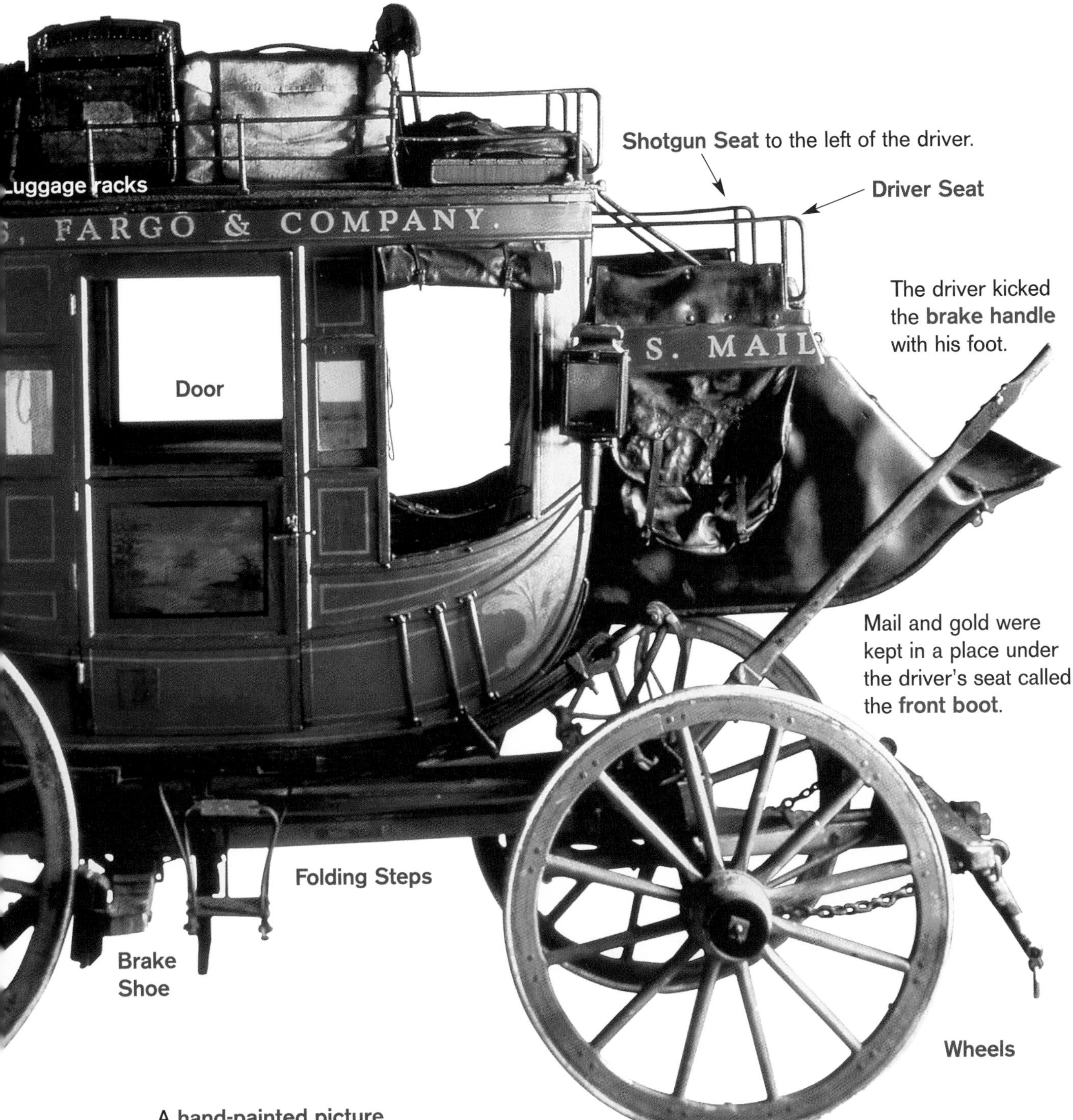

Luggage racks

FARGO & COMPANY.

Door

Shotgun Seat to the left of the driver.

Driver Seat

The driver kicked the **brake handle** with his foot.

S. MAIL

Mail and gold were kept in a place under the driver's seat called the **front boot**.

Folding Steps

Brake Shoe

Wheels

A **hand-painted picture** decorated the coach door, usually featuring a landscape, an eagle, or a famous person.

The coach's base, or **undercarriage**, was often painted yellow, which hid the dust of the road.

Andy's Diary

Central Overland Trail, Nebraska Territory   April 1, 1860

So far, our journey has been like a relay race. Each team of horses races as fast as it can for a short time. When the horses get to the next station, they are replaced by a fresh team.

At the last station, stablehands rushed out as soon as the coach arrived. They led away the old horses and hooked up the new ones. In less than 15 minutes, we were off again!

Heading West in a Stagecoach

What was it like to ride a stagecoach from the East to the West? Imagine being cooped up with eight other people for almost a month. In a full coach, each person had only 15 inches of seat space.

For 25 days, you and your fellow passengers would sway and bounce across endless prairie, windy mountain peaks, or blazing deserts. By the time you got to California, you might be really tired of your fellow passengers, or they might have become your closest friends.

Stagecoaches rolled day and night, so people learned to sleep sitting up. During the day, passengers swapped stories, read, tried to write letters, or looked at the scenery and wild animals they passed.

How should you behave on a stagecoach?

A newspaper published "Hints for Plains Travelers" in 1877:

1. When the driver asks you to get out and walk, do it without grumbling.

2. Don't growl at the food; stage companies generally provide the best they can.

3. Don't flop over on your neighbor when sleeping.

4. Don't ask how far it is to the next station until you get there.

5. Don't discuss politics or religion, nor point out places on the road where horrible murders have been committed.

What would you pack?

Each person was allowed 25 pounds of baggage. Most people brought clothes, blankets, water canteens, and weapons.

What would you eat?

Most stagecoach stations were far from any town. They usually served bread, beans, pork, and mush (thick cornmeal porridge).

On the Great Plains of eastern Colorado   May 15, 1862

    I was sleeping soundly until Betsy woke me. "Listen!" she said. First I heard a low rumble like thunder. Pushing aside the curtain and peering outside the coach, I saw a huge cloud. Was another storm brewing? The driver's shout answered my question: "Buffalo ahead!"

Natural Obstacles in the West

    To get to California, stagecoaches had to cross the Great Plains and the mountains. Passengers, drivers, and horses struggled with many natural hazards along the way.

    In the summer, the Great Plains were hot, dry, and dusty. Streams and waterholes dried up. Passengers were careful to fill their canteens whenever water appeared. Often it was hundreds of miles to the next source of water.

    Millions of buffalo roamed the Great Plains in enormous herds. When they stampeded, they might trample everything in their path. To scare off the animals, stagecoach drivers fired their guns to turn the herd away from the coach. After traveling for days across the Great Plains, travelers cheered when they caught sight of the mountains.

In the Rocky Mountains and the Sierra Nevadas, driving a stagecoach was dangerous. Steep, narrow trails and frequent rockslides could send horses, coach, and passengers over a cliff.

Climbing up a mountain was only half the battle. When the horses started down, they had to brace against the full weight of the coach pushing them forward. If the stagecoach went too fast, it could crash and overturn. The travelers might have to walk many miles to the next waystation.

Blinding snowstorms added another hazard to mountain travel. Inside the unheated coaches, the temperature often fell below zero. Passengers huddled under buffalo robes to keep warm.

Nathanial's Diary

On the Great Plains   October 7, 1863

Today, at about noon, we saw several people on horseback. Mr. Walker said they were Indians and loaded his gun.

The hair on the back of my neck stood up as I watched the group halt at the top of the hill. I could see rifles across their saddles. One rider galloped down the hill toward us. He had only a bow slung across his back. Mr. Walker cocked his gun and moved toward the window to shoot him.

"Wait!" I shouted and pushed the gun down. I could see that the boy wasn't much older than I am. He rode up beside the coach and stuck his head right in the window. When he saw me, he stared at me in surprise. Then we both grinned. I knew if I lived here, he'd be my friend.

The Clash of Cultures

Travelers heading west heard terrifying stories about western native people who raided stagecoaches and scalped passengers. Some Native Americans did attack coaches. They rode off with guns, food, and often the horses. The Native Americans, however, were struggling to keep their way of life.

On the Great Plains, Native Americans usually hunted the buffalo, which provided them with meat and hides for food, clothing, and shelter. Following the roaming buffalo herds, they traveled far across the plains.

Settlers moving west crossed buffalo hunting grounds. Sometimes, they came into conflict with the Native American hunters.

Most Native Americans were not hostile or dangerous. Many westward travelers found that the native peoples often helped them.

Native Americans knew the land much better than the newcomers. They served as guides and helped travelers find their way across the vast unmarked plains and along confusing mountain trails. They also taught settlers about local foods and wildlife.

Central Overland Road, Utah Territory   September 8, 1866

We met our new driver today. He strode over to us, pulling on his leather gloves, his whip stuck under his arm. I looked up into his unsmiling face. Then he laughed. "Howdy," he said. "Want to ride up front?"

It was tricky getting up onto the box. I climbed from the hub of the big front wheel to its rim. Then I rocked the whole coach as I hoisted myself into the seat beside the driver. We were really high up!

Stagecoach drivers had as much power as ship captains. They were responsible for horses, stagecoaches, cargo, and human lives. Passengers, station keepers, and stablehands respected drivers for their expert skills.

Stagecoach Drivers: Legends in Their Day

Hank Monk gained fame after he drove writer Horace Greeley to Placerville, California, on time to give an important speech. Monk drove his coach at breakneck speed through the countryside. Inside, Greeley was tossed and bounced. At one especially big bump, Greeley's head broke right through the roof of the coach! He arrived in Placerville red-faced and rumpled, but he was on time, thanks to Hank Monk.

Charley Parkhurst was a fearless driver. On one trip, Charley reached a bridge over a raging river. Surging waters crashed so hard that the bridge shook. Another driver might have turned around, but Charley cracked his whip and sent the team onto the shaking bridge. Just as the coach got across, the bridge collapsed into the water.

Charley was famous for two reasons — his bravery as a driver and the fact that he was actually a woman in disguise! Charley disguised herself as a man so she could be a stagecoach driver.

Charley Parkhurst

Drivers held three reins in each hand.

Another famous and fearless driver was "Stagecoach Mary Fields." Mary was the first African American woman to carry the United States mail. Nothing could stop the mail on Mary Fields's route, not even outlaws. When bandits attacked her coach, Mary switched all six reins to one hand and fired her six-shooter with the other, racing along at full speed until the bandits gave up.

Daniel's Diary

Outside Havilah, California　　　　　　　　　**September 9, 1867**

Our coach slowed to a crawl as the horses started up the hill. Suddenly, three masked figures rode out from the bushes. One grabbed the reins of the frightened horses, while another aimed his rifle at the guard. The third bandit pulled up in front of the horses, pointed a gun at our driver, and yelled, "Throw down the box!"

Bandits!

A stagecoach carrying gold faced the risk of a robbery. Bandits would stop a stagecoach to steal the gold and money that might be in the strongbox under the driver's seat. Sometimes, bandits also robbed the passengers and stole the mail, which contained money the miners were sending to their families. An armed guard, called a shotgun rider, sat up top with the driver for protection.

REWARD

WELLS, FARGO & CO.'S EXPRESS BOX
on SONORA AND MILTON STAGE ROUTE, was ROBBED this morning, near Reynolds' Ferry, by one man, masked and armed with sixteen shooter and double-barreled shot gun. We will pay

$250

for ARREST and CONVICTION of the Robber.

JNO. J. VALENTINE, Genl Supt.

San Francisco, July 26, 1875.

One notorious bandit was Black Bart. Wearing a flour sack over his head, Bart waved a shotgun at the driver and demanded the treasure box. Over a period of eight years, Black Bart single-handedly robbed 27 Wells Fargo stagecoaches. Sometimes, he made fun of Wells Fargo detectives by leaving a poem near the empty strongbox.

One Wells Fargo detective vowed to capture Black Bart. For years, he followed every clue without success. Finally, in 1883, Black Bart accidentally dropped a handkerchief during a robbery. The detective traced the laundry mark on the handkerchief through 91 laundries, until he found his man. The dangerous robber turned out to be a soft-spoken man who lived in a hotel in San Francisco when he wasn't holding up stagecoaches. His gun was never loaded. Black Bart served a long term in prison, then disappeared without a trace.

Black Bart considered himself a poet ("po8") and liked to leave a taunting poem at the scene of the crime.

Beth's Diary

Grass Valley, California

June 6, 1868

"Coming into Grass Valley!" our driver roared. Everyone pushed to look out of the window. A tiny speck on the horizon quickly turned into a row of buildings with wooden sidewalks. As we rolled down the main street, children ran alongside the coach shouting and waving.

Our stagecoach pulled up in front of the post office. Huge clouds of dust settled as we staggered out of the coach. As my feet touched the ground, I felt dizzy. I couldn't see much because of the dust, and strange voices surrounded me. Suddenly, large hands lifted me off the ground.

"You made it!" Pa shouted in my ear, hugging me tight and laughing. "Welcome to California!"

In small towns, the arrival of a stagecoach was cause for celebration. Cheering men shot their guns in the air, while excited townspeople flocked around the coach to greet the travelers and to look for mail and packages.

The Coming of the Railroad

The years from 1857 to 1868 were the highpoint of stagecoaching in the West. Jaunty red and yellow Concord Coaches rolled west and east, connecting the country.

From the windows of the stagecoaches, though, passengers could see the signs of the future. Railroad tracks were being laid.

Two companies raced to build the first transcontinental railroad. One started laying tracks from the East. The other started from the West. On May 10, 1869, the two tracks met at Promontory Point, Utah. People cheered and shot off cannons as the two tracks were connected with a golden spike.

Trains now started carrying mail and passengers across the country, putting transcontinental stagecoaches out of business. The "iron horses" sped night and day, reaching speeds that real horses could never achieve. A single train could carry far more passengers, goods, and mail than the largest stagecoach.

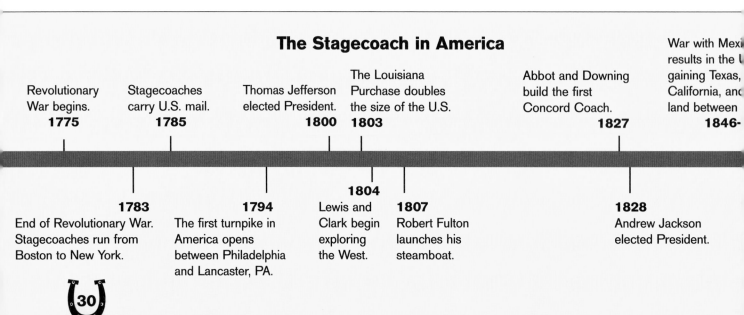

The Stagecoach in America

Revolutionary War begins. **1775**	Stagecoaches carry U.S. mail. **1785**	Thomas Jefferson elected President. **1800**	The Louisiana Purchase doubles the size of the U.S. **1803**		Abbot and Downing build the first Concord Coach. **1827**	War with Mexi results in the l gaining Texas, California, and land between **1846-**

1783 End of Revolutionary War. Stagecoaches run from Boston to New York.	**1794** The first turnpike in America opens between Philadelphia and Lancaster, PA.	**1804** Lewis and Clark begin exploring the West.	**1807** Robert Fulton launches his steamboat.		**1828** Andrew Jackson elected President.

The Stagecoach Today

Stagecoaches continued to roll because the railroad did not go to every town. They remained important until automobiles became popular. In 1910, the last stagecoach company closed, ending an important era in American transportation.

Today, the stagecoach appears in movies, art, and stories. In many museums, you can see real stagecoaches, along with clothes, money, tickets, and letters that belonged to the original passengers. In the Wells Fargo History Museum, for example, you can see gold dust and strongboxes from over 100 years ago. You can even sit inside a Concord Coach.

As you are zooming along in a car, bus, or plane, imagine what the journey would have been like 150 years ago. There were a lot more dangers back then, but there were also a lot more adventures. Would you have more fun traveling in 1852, or traveling in 2002? It depends on your point of view.

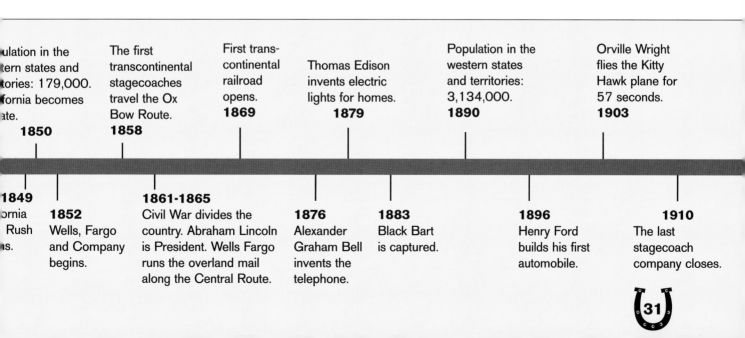

ulation in the tern states and tories: 179,000. fornia becomes ate.
1850

The first transcontinental stagecoaches travel the Ox Bow Route.
1858

First transcontinental railroad opens.
1869

Thomas Edison invents electric lights for homes.
1879

Population in the western states and territories: 3,134,000.
1890

Orville Wright flies the Kitty Hawk plane for 57 seconds.
1903

1849
ornia
Rush
is.

1852
Wells, Fargo and Company begins.

1861-1865
Civil War divides the country. Abraham Lincoln is President. Wells Fargo runs the overland mail along the Central Route.

1876
Alexander Graham Bell invents the telephone.

1883
Black Bart is captured.

1896
Henry Ford builds his first automobile.

1910
The last stagecoach company closes.

Index

ART CREDITS:
   The illustrations on the following pages were created by A. Richard Mansir: **1:** *The Concord Coach*; **2:** *Travel by Night*; **3:** *Through the Countryside*; **4:** *Stuck in the Mud*; **7:** *A Wayside Inn*; *Inn Sign*; **8:** *Blaze*; **12:** *The Butterfield Mail*; **13:** *Major Overland Stage Routes*; **19:** *Inside the Coach*; **21:** *Mountain Pass in a Blizzard*; **22:** *The Buffalo Hunt*; **27:** *Throw Down the Box!*; **28-29:** *The Stagecoach Arrives*.
   The illustrations and photographs on the following pages are the property of Wells Fargo Bank and used with express permission: **front cover:** *The Best Leads* by William Tipton; **6:** Letter from 1840; **9:** *Over the High Road* by William Tipton; **10:** Gold nuggets and $50 gold piece; **11:** *Stagecoach Passing Mt. Shasta* by Aaron Stein; **14:** "Great Overland Mail Route" poster; Henry Wells; William G. Fargo; **15:** The "Henry" rifle; Colt's Patent Revolver; **16-17:** Photograph of an Abbot-Downing Coach by Tom Vano; **18:** *Gold Country* by Keith Christie; **19:** Traveling trunks; **20:** Buffalo; **21:** *Coach Overturned* by Charles M. Russel, from *Fifteen Thousand Miles by Stage*, by Carrie A. Strahorn, 1911; **23:** *Perils of the Overland Trail* by H.W. Hansen; **24:** Stagecoach driving through water; **25:** Charlie Parkhurst; Driver's reins; **26:** Reward poster; Open strongbox; **27:** Black Bart; **30-31:** *An Express-Freight Shipment of 30 Coaches April 15, 1868 from Abbot, Downing & Co., Concord, N.H., to Wells, Fargo Co., Omaha, Neb.* by John Borgum; **32:** Coach at sunset; **back cover:** *Winter Run* by Keith Christie.
   The photograph of the stage station on page **19** is used with permission from the San Diego Historical Society Photograph Collection.